Unearthing Sunlight

Rina Begum

Presentation by *BookLeaf Publishing*

Web: www.bookleafpub.com

E-mail: info@bookleafpub.com

ISBN: 9789395087360

First edition 2022

Contents

Roots

We tried burying our roots
hiding them beneath the ground,
but the brown in our skin grew
darker when the sky split
asunder, and their thunderous
words came thrashing down.
Do you see how we slowly sink
deep and deeper into ourselves?
For stormy days hurl our spirits
so gradually we begin to drown…
Notice how the Earth would churn
when we wilt and wither away
but our roots refuse to let us rot
as we steadily rise above our skin
and claim Nature as ours today.

Dystopia

Drunken on fear,
they slowly lose their morality
never sober enough to see
in these eyes, our humanity.

Living in a skin
painted in melanin is our sin
but as children of Adam,
surely are we not all kin?

Humankind has been carved
by God with the same clay
yet why ours a dark brown
like the dirt on Earth I pray.

We did not forsee Dystopia
would be a part of God's plan
as we exist alongside Monsters,
masked in the image of Man.

Oh the irony! Lusting for 'purity'
has made them unholy
Oh, for the love of God!
How this desire devours us slowly...

They grab hold of our tongue,
mercilessly tearing it out

Your Truth is one the world
could do without.

They slit our body open
to spit at the 'devil' within
You should return to the Earth
where God found your skin.

Only Red seeps through,
tainting their sacred lands
Look at our blood-stained tears,
their blood-stained hands!

Melanin

Our Melanin skin glistens
like the Earth that is drenched
by clouds which break into rainfall,
or as though stars have shed their dust
onto our God-blessed skin,
but it is Sunlight that sinks deep,
leaving our skin enriched in beauty;
deep brown, sun-tanned, majestic.

Water Lilies

5

Mother Nature's womb is lined with stardust,
she gives birth to starry flowers that emerge
from the Earth's skin, drinking the Sun's glory…
The Heavens cry in awe of her flowering plants,
they see her lilies glow like a majestic jewel
But no matter where the waters drift them away,
their thick stems stay rooted to their Motherland.

Turbulent Waves

Like the vastness of oceanic waters,
we write volumes on the turbulence of life,
how it leaves a bitterness on our tongues
and rubs salt upon our open cut wounds.

We struggle in vain to catch our breath
when we are down under in deep waters,
where we are overcome by waves of sorrow
that sweep sinking souls away into gloom…

Yet from the depths of despair we still rise,
we swim towards the distant liquid Sun
whilst rippling waves of hope encircle us,
soothing us with the same devastating touch.

And how often have we found ourselves
always drawn back to the edge of land,
so our eyes can drink in the Ocean view
to make our vision clear like oceanic blue.

Ecstasy

Free my soul and feed it your Love,
for this distance creates hunger
and my heart remains dry.
In ecstasy, my eyes flow with Love
but you bring forth Oceans –
I am left sinking gracefully,
drowning happily, deep
into your midst and out of solitude.

The Deep Blue

Cold sea air wraps around my soul,
do I dare call it a state of euphoria
to be suffocated by fierce winds?
Living has never felt so real
until breathing becomes heavy!
inhale...exhale…inhale...exhale…
He enters my body, and clutches
onto my heart with his bare hands

one. two. three. four. fi…
and like a gentle breeze that awakens
the hairs of the skin, he releases me
I was his to crush, and with one
strong blow he could do it
but how to merely hold my heart
gave him power over me.
His howl drowns into a whisper
his voice now drained by the Sea…

The cold water underneath my feet
tickles me, tempting me to join his abode.
The waves soar in the distance
till they shrink as they approach me,
and bow down at my feet: why,
Nature has a strange way of greeting
Humankind when our paths cross.
I accepted the invitation and now

I was the one doing the entering –

His vastness, I could not transcend
for it only reaffirmed my transience.
Only through defiance of natural laws
my fear of falling into the Deep Blue
would dissolve, so there I was –
making waves, navigating myself in
the depths of his soul without a compass
as I floated on with the flow of the current

Hazel Green Eyes

Love looks towards me
with his hazel green eyes
and I am lost in the depths
of his golden, earthy green forest.

It is in that streak of hazel
that Sunlight flashes before me
and I watch the Sun rise
in his elusive yet endearing eyes.

My cheeks tingle and tint,
as his every glance is a caress
and the roses he plants in my skin
blossom on my sun-kissed face.

A Rose

You presented me a rose
thinking it romantic. I smiled,
feeling its weight upon my heart
how could I claim a part of Nature
within my hands like a conqueror?

Am I to accept it as a token of
your conquered love for me?

Mother Nature moans,
she hears the cries of her offspring
as I choke its life between the palm
of my hands. Human touch
only knows to destroy, so I plead
guilty to a crime I am yet to commit.

I will rob her of her child,
I will not bathe it in sunlight
nor will I quench its thirst.

The rose that once stood erect in
the fertile soil of Mother Nature's womb
will be crushed to scattered petals,
into ashes, because this heart
does not know how to feel…

But Ahh! It bites into my skin,

its teeth stained with my blood,
as it escapes from my clutches
proud of its heinous deed.

My eyes are cast to the ground,
as Mother Nature once again
ascends to her Throne.

The Touch of Mankind

Mother Nature has fallen into the shadows,
I fear she has been suffering in silence
after the reigns of Earth were usurped
from her hands. I see her solemn face
everywhere I turn – dull, grey and dark
clouds of circles around her lifeless eyes.
Mother Nature stares at me with those
talking eyes, *how easily do you turn away?*

Mother Nature is afraid for her friends
in the wild. Mankind is unafraid to use force
when he wishes; he cuts, saws, chops in a
downward force, so down they fall, and turn
into embers, into ashes, into dust. Mother Nature
struggles to breathe, choking and constantly
coughing, she gasps for air. She sighs,
there is no comfort but anxiety in his touch.

Mother Nature is losing her nurturing touch.
Stricken with sickness, I watch her weaken,
her stomach congested with leftovers
of yesterday. No volume of water can
flush out the waste, as the toxins flow in
and through her veins. Her children left
homeless. Mother Nature worries,
Fertility must be a crime in a body like mine.

All of a sudden, Mankind is forced to go
into hibernation, to hide away from the
misdoings of selfish hands. We all witness
Mother Nature reclaim her reigns as she
greets Earth with her nurturing hands. In awe,
Mankind observes how she flourishes
in his absence; smiling as she inhales the
fresh air, Mother Nature welcomes back her
children and cries, *I will always be your home.*

Sunsets

I watched you set fire to the sky,
saw its skin rip open, bursting with
lustrous lights that covered the horizon,
like how lava breaks from Earth's shackles
smothering its skin with a sinister touch.
The alighted sky brought me pleasure,
I felt ashamed to feel enlightened
by an act that appeared to be sadistic.
The sky was left wounded –I could
not fathom how something like this
could look so destructively beautiful...
But what you created did not feel like art,
and are Sunsets not a beauty of Nature?
Now I see, there are no skies you have ignited
but my heart you have used as your canvas:
here are no Sunsets, but a fire within my chest.

A Fiery Touch

Fear the Female who speaks
with fire in her mouth,
for a fiery touch has set
her dancing spirit in flames,
so she burns in the sky
like the Sun, never dying,
but blazing bright, as a beacon
for those turned into ashes.

The Fearsome One

When you look upon Nature,
Do you dare to curse her gender?

When she lies down flat like a field,
Do you find her form offensive?
It is in that fertile soil of her womb
that seeds are sown, so see how her
skin stretches, making space for a burst
of new life to breathe within her being

When she bleeds Sunsets into the sky,
Do you then realise the beauty of Nature?
It is the same red that streams between
her limbs; the same red that spills the
flower beds when she is caressed; the
same red that flows when she gives birth

When she bathes herself in sunshine,
Do you think her bare skin is threatening?
It is Nature's undressing when she sheds
her leaves, she shrivels and shrinks and
grows into a new skin, awakening in
the new spring, blossoming in full bloom.

Eclipse

When we collide we are the Sun and the Moon
catching a glimpse of each other in orbit
only has life slowly slipped from my lips
when they have met with yours…
but like the way night greets day with a kiss,
in this way you resuscitate me –
Our breathing inconstant, as the rhythm
of our heartbeats intertwine.

Are we not masters of Love;
conductors of the melody running through
our veins; an orchestra consisting of you and me.
How carefully into the darkness we disappear…
I bring light to your hands, and how strikingly
it carves an Eclipse of our union,
a sight you have sought in your courting –
a picturesque scene!

A hit of my rays, and you watch this star
burn in the sky; exposed, bare, but
with your embrace you keep it aflame, alive.
An alignment in our paths and we trigger
the order of things. We took time into our hands
and painted our image across the horizon…
so in all the beginnings, and in every ending,
we will be reminded –

Our Love does not fade when we are apart.

Head in the Clouds

My mind wandered among the clouds,
traversing the skies of my imagination
kisses of sunshine fall upon my skin
as I am embraced by the Sun's glory
and left lovesick when I am without it.
I cannot but fear my fall to Earth
to be tragic and inevitable like Icarus...
A heavy mist coats the sky below-
a great grey cloud of uncertainty,
that overshadows any ray of Light
peering from the Heavens above.
But I know the blue skies up here
will also lose their comforting colour
as they too will become shadowed
by the intrusion of a fierce storm.
Melancholy, I watch the passing clouds
how merrily they glide through the sky.
Is there any wonder I wish I too
could be like the clouds, who sleep
and wake with bliss and in beauty.

A Dark Cloud

Are there blue skies that do not die?

How often they all gradually perish,
choking in the overbearing Darkness
by a kind of grey smoldering smoke,
that hangs haughtily over my head.

The rain soaks into my fragile skin,
flooding profusely in my corrupt veins
drowning has become regular exercise,
my feeble body is forced to undertake.

How the Sun shines in a distant horizon
but warmth never grazes upon my skin
so hairs on my skin stay and stand erect
for coldness never knows when to leave

Can it be that sleep is my only escape
from such a sleepless and soulless storm?
Maybe then that can stop the Sea of rain
overflowing from my cloud-like eyes.

Black Holes

How do you bring back sunshine to eyes
that hold Black Holes within them?

The Sun sleeps on,
so I have forgotten the taste of Sunlight,
how it seeps through the cracks
of the empty shell I wear
and dispels the Darkness out
of my shadowed soul,
like the way daylight creeps through
the canopy in the break of dawn
illuminating the depths of the forlorn forest.

But Light has learnt not to linger
in hollow places,
where it would be met with a fearful fate
to flicker and fizzle out,
like a burning flame in an open campfire
which surrenders to the clasp of a chilly breeze
no warmth, no glimmer of hope,
just the growing Black Hole within my chest,
ready to extinguish any ray of Light
and turn it into Nothingness.

Reviving the Light

When I close my eyes
I am snatched away
by the Darkness
gone forever
never revived
but I have learnt
to live alongside Death
who creeps on me,
lurking
in the shadows
of my mind.
I feel as if I cannot feel
I talk but never of sense
my thoughts provide
no comfort
there is no refuge,
I know.

When I open my eyes
the sky is a reminder
of my end
because she too slips
into it – the Darkness,
a kind of unconsciousness.
When I look at her
I cannot say she is alive,
she resembles too much

of the emptiness
that never leaves me,
that stays with me.
How the Moon stares
at me, so I stare
back at him, but
what are his eyes
telling me?

Those eyes;
why do I feel as if
I've seen that glisten
somewhere else,
in someone else?
I blink, I cannot look
away, but I cannot
unsee it either,
so I force it shut
till it disappears
and how curiously
it does
and how slowly
it destroys me;
the Darkness has never
been more blinding,
it only knows
how to swallow me
whole, so I fall again…

but I am awaken –
suddenly; shaken; remembering
seeing that same glimmer in my eyes.

A Search for a Starry Night

I could not find stars in the midnight sky
so I would be devoured by the Darkness.

You could not feel an embrace more chilling,
more unsettling, than an embrace from Death
my eyes search for a struggling glimmer
of Light to pierce the soul of the dark abyss

Instead I discover depth hidden between
the brush streaks across the empty canvas
waves of swirling blues; sapphire, space, steel;
the Throne of night painted in their shadow

An unearthly silence, a broken stillness
and a sight so serene unveils itself...
In a cloudless sky they came like fireflies
that solemn night died before it began.

The Majestic God

The stars, the planets, and all the universe
with everything in it, exists as evidence
of the Majesty of God. If it was not for His
Divine decree, stars would defy nature
by shooting down onto earth, as to prostrate
in His presence; they would burn away
their existence, by burying themselves into
the skins of earth where no trace would
be left behind - as if they were not once alive…

and all that would remain is the face of God

An Existential Crisis

Maybe all we are, are mere particles
travelling, scattering, and dying
as we dance in the display of iridescent lights;
blues, reds, purples; or is black all we see?

Then to what matter is named a Universe–
are we not particles holding an entire
Universe within ourselves?

Our being transcends our physical entity–
we are not defined by the atoms
that make our existence a reality,
but the energy floating around us
and the forces gravitating us
together and apart.

We want to be expanding–
growing into a star,
forming a part of a constellation,
or even becoming whole Galaxies.

Feel how this energy inside of us burns,
it burns as gamma rays wait to leap out;
though if we don't allow these rays
to be emitted, how can our Light
truly transcend?

See how this space between us
this emptiness, is All consuming–
we are falling
falling
falling
into the Black Hole.

It is inevitable, we are to be pulled
and there is no force to pull us away.

So what are we…

Maybe all we are, are mere particles
but is it enough to simply exist?
For Time has us bound and the Universe
is awaiting our arrival and our end.

'*Unearthing Sunlight*' is a debut collection of eloquent and enthralling poems. This poetry uses the natural world to explore how the female spirit navigates herself in matters of the heart and mind. Beneath the poet's use of layered language, there are deeper meanings to be unearthed that reveal issues such as mental illness, racism, and trauma – all of which trouble one's identity and self-perception. Each poem will take you to different moments of day and night, as you find that hope is never lost as long as the sun rises.

ABOUT THE AUTHOR

Rina Begum is a British Bangladeshi poet, who transforms ordinary prose into her own poetic voice and writes about abstract ideas, the human experience and the natural world. She also teaches English Language and Literature at a secondary school. Her poetry has been influenced by poets that she has grown up reading, such as Wordsworth, Rumi, and Shakespeare. Rina wishes her poetry will bring new meaning to her life and others, as she believes that it is a language that is deep rooted within us all, and has the power to ignite minds.

Cover design by Lavleen Vaz

Milton Keynes UK
Ingram Content Group UK Ltd.
UKHW020630070823
426447UK00017B/1082